ROBERT FULTON

From Submarine to Steamboat

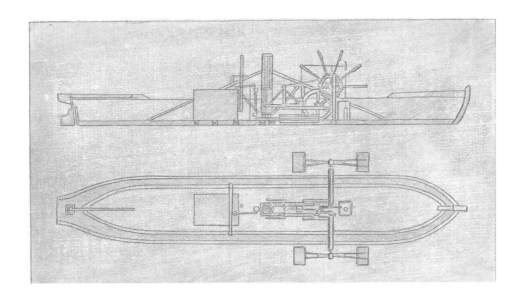

ROBERT FULTON

From Submarine to Steamboat

by **Steven Kroll**

illustrated by
Bill Farnsworth

Holiday House/New York

Robert Fulton was born on a farm outside Lancaster, Pennsylvania, on November 14, 1765. After six hard years, Robert's father, a tailor by trade, gave up farming and moved the family back to Lancaster. Three years later, he died.

Robert attended a strict Quaker school and was always in trouble. Then, one day, a classmate brought in some paints mixed in mussel shells. Robert borrowed them and painted so well the boy gave him the whole set. A little later, Robert began painting signs for local tradesmen.

In April 1775, the American Revolution began, and Lancaster became a supply center for the Continental army. Robert started visiting the local gunsmiths' shops. Urged to submit drawings and designs, he had designed an air gun by 1779.

The Fulton family remained poor. At about seventeen, Robert
was apprenticed to Jeremiah Andrews, a jeweler in Philadelphia.
There he wove hair into patterns for jewelry and began painting
miniatures on chips of ivory.

By early 1786, Robert may have come down with tuberculosis. At the same time, his mother wanted to move back to the country. Always a problem solver, he borrowed money and bought a farm in Hopewell Township, Washington County. Then he went off to Bath, Virginia, a fashionable spa, to recover.

In Bath, Robert probably met James Rumsey. Rumsey was experimenting, using steam to pump water in at the bow of a boat and drive it through a pipe out the stern. But Robert was still more interested in art than in steamboats and wanted to go to Europe to study painting.

Robert returned to Philadelphia and opened his own miniature-painting and hair-working shop a block from the Delaware River. Late in the summer of 1787, during the Constitutional Convention, he sailed for Europe to study art. Before he left, he might have seen wild-eyed John Fitch's first serious steamboat bucking the Delaware current on August 22.

While living in Philadelphia, Robert had met Benjamin Franklin. He arrived in London carrying a letter of introduction from Franklin to Benjamin West, court painter to King George III. West had grown up near Lancaster. He helped Robert find lodgings and took him on as a student.

Meanwhile, Fulton became friendly with the duke of Bridgewater, who had built his own canal, and the earl of Stanhope, a great experimenter. Inspired by their work, Fulton abandoned art for civil engineering between 1792 and 1794. He planned small systems of canals to transport goods inland and designed machines for cutting marble and spinning flax. He also corresponded with Lord Stanhope about a steam-powered boat that would imitate the movement of a salmon's tail.

Nothing succeeded. In the spring of 1797, during a lull in the wars between France and England, Fulton went to Paris determined to find someone to back his canal schemes. There he became friends with Joel Barlow, a poet and businessman, and his wife, Ruth. For the next seven years, he would live with the Barlows in their home across from the Luxembourg Gardens.

Meanwhile, Fulton was writing about ending war. Convinced that destroying navies was a step toward that end, he designed a submarine, a weapon no navy could oppose.

Although Fulton never admitted his submarine was not totally original, its principles, if not its appearance, were based on the *American Turtle*, a fascinating failure created by David Bushnell during the American Revolution. Both boats pumped water in for submerging and out for surfacing, but the *Turtle* held only one man and looked like two tortoise shells pressed together on end. Fulton's *Nautilus* would hold three men. It was shaped like a long oval with a sail that could be folded down and covered.

Fulton pestered the French government for approval on his submarine, but got nowhere. Needing money, he acquired the French rights to a "panorama," a huge dome with a giant painting around the inside. As his version, he had *The Burning of Moscow* painted. It opened early in 1800 and was his first big financial success.

That money, plus a contribution from Joel Barlow, helped Fulton build the *Nautilus*. He ran underwater trials, but two attempts to sink British ships failed. The French government was not convinced.

Meanwhile, in 1801, Robert Fulton met the American minister to France, Robert R. Livingston. A wealthy landowner, Livingston was a former chancellor of New York State. He, too, was interested in steamboats and had been granted the right to control all such traffic in New York State waters.

On October 10, 1802, the two men became business partners. Livingston then persuaded the New York legislature to extend his right for twenty years. To keep it, he and Fulton would have to run a twenty-ton boat at four miles per hour on the Hudson River within the first two years.

Others had come close to creating a profitable steamboat, among them Scotland's William Symington in March 1803 and John Fitch, whose rear paddle-wheel boat had run more than six thousand miles on the Delaware River in 1790. Fulton studied them all. His first steamboat sank in a storm on the river Seine in July 1803, because the French engine was too heavy for the frame. But on August 9 a sturdier version, with two large paddle wheels mounted on an axle like a cart, succeeded.

Abolishing war was still on Fulton's mind. Since 1801 he had been secretly sending information about his submarine and torpedo schemes to friends in Great Britain in the hope that that country might finance his efforts. In addition, he wanted an English-made Boulton and Watt steam engine, the best in the world with its separate condenser for cooling the steam, for his New York steamboat. Because England and France were at war, the Birmingham-built engines were not allowed out of England. If Fulton were working for the British government, matters might be different.

He had meetings with a British agent, the mysterious "Mr. Smith," in Amsterdam and Paris, but it wasn't until July 20, 1804, that Fulton, now back in London, had a deal to develop a torpedo-delivery system for the British. The effort failed. It was time to return to America.

Allowed to bring along a Boulton and Watt engine, Fulton arrived in New York on December 13, 1806, visited the Barlows in Washington, D.C., and got back to steamboats.

Charles Brownne built a wooden hull for the new boat at Corlear's Hook on the East River in New York City. Then Fulton had it towed to his workshop at Paulus Hook Ferry on the Hudson River. Work was slow, and guards had to be hired for protection against riverboatmen, angry that steam might destroy their livelihood. Also time had already run out. Livingston had to get a two-year extension from the legislature.

The Steamboat looked odd. Nicknamed "Fulton's Folly," it was 150 feet long, but only 13 feet wide, with a square stern and tuck. The deck rose only a few feet above the water. There was a mast at the rear for sails and in the middle, in full view, the steam engine and a chimney. Two paddle wheels hung over the sides.

On August 17, 1807, *The Steamboat*'s first voyage, from near State's Prison, New York City, to Albany, began. It was a hot summer day. About forty stylish passengers, most of them Livingstons, were on board. Heading north, the steamboat looked like "a sawmill mounted on a raft and set on fire."

After a night on the Hudson, the boat reached Clermont, the Livingston estate. Chancellor Livingston rose and spoke. Before the end of the century, he predicted, steamboats would cross the ocean. What's more, Robert Fulton was going to marry his niece, Harriet!

The passengers stayed at Clermont overnight and arrived in Albany to cheers at five o'clock the following afternoon. The steamboat had gone 150 miles in 32 hours. By contrast, New York to Albany sloops and schooners usually took four days.

But people still wondered if Fulton's steamboat could replace the sailboats. On September 4, after two weeks of repairs and improvements, *The Steamboat* carried fourteen passengers on its first commercial voyage to Albany. By November 19, when the boat was laid up for the winter, it had turned a profit.

Robert Fulton had not invented the steamboat, but he was the first to combine the right features and produce a commercial success. After its first season, however, the boat, now called *The North River*, had to be rebuilt. The new version became a model for future steamboats: a heavier, wider "floating palace," with three cabins, fifty-four berths, a kitchen, and a bar.

Meanwhile, on January 7, 1808, Fulton had married Harriet Livingston. She bore four children. He continued to build new boats (a total of twenty-one) and brought steamboats to the Mississippi River with his *New Orleans*. He also built ferries to cross the Hudson and East Rivers. During the War of 1812, he convinced Congress to let him build the first steam warship, *The Demologos*.

Unfortunately, the lung trouble from Fulton's youth returned in 1812. A few years later, in January 1815, he went to Trenton, New Jersey, to testify about steamboat rights. Coming back with him, racing for a late ferry, his lawyer, Thomas Emmet, fell through the ice. Somehow Fulton rescued him, but arrived home very ill. On February 23, 1815, he died.

After an enormous funeral procession, Robert Fulton was buried in the Livingston family vault at Trinity Church, New York City. Shops and offices closed, as Americans mourned a man whose technical skills, artistry, and perseverance had changed the way they lived.

Important Dates

November 14, 1765	Robert Fulton is born on a farm in Little Britain, Pennsylvania.
Around 1782	Robert is apprenticed to Jeremiah Andrews, an English jeweler with a shop in Philadelphia.
Summer, 1787	Robert sails for Europe to study art.
Between 1792 and 1794	Robert abandons art for civil engineering.
Early 1800	Robert opens his successful "panorama" in Paris. He and Joel Barlow finance the building of his submarine, the *Nautilus.*
October 10, 1802	Robert Fulton and Robert R. Livingston form a partnership to build a steamboat.
August 9, 1803	After his first steamboat sinks in the river Seine, Robert succeeds with his rebuilt version.
December 13, 1806	Still a failure after almost twenty years abroad, Robert arrives in New York.
August 9, 1807	Four years to the day after Robert's first successful steamboat trial on the Seine, his new boat has a test run on the Lower Hudson River.
August 17	The first voyage of *The Steamboat,* also called *The North River,* from North River, near State's Prison, New York City, to Albany.
September 4	*The Steamboat's* first commercial voyage to Albany, with fourteen passengers.
January 7, 1808	Robert Fulton marries Harriet Livingston.
January 1815	Thomas Emmet, Robert's lawyer, falls through the ice on the Hudson River. Robert rescues him but becomes very ill.
February 23	Robert Fulton dies. The next day he is buried in the Livingston family vault at Trinity Church, New York City.

Acknowledgments
The author wishes to thank Dr. Vincent DiGirolamo
of Colgate University for his help in establishing the "best truth"
about Robert Fulton's life and work in more than one instance.

Author's Note

Many history books call Robert Fulton's first Hudson River steamboat the *Clermont*, but Fulton never called it that. On its first voyage, he called it simply *The Steamboat*. In later advertisements, it became *The North River Steamboat*. After the rebuilding of 1807–1808, the boat had to be registered as a new vessel. In his application, but nowhere else, Fulton referred to *The North River Steamboat of Clermont*. Mostly he just called it *The North River*.

Before James Watt appeared, the most advanced steam engine had been the one built by Thomas Newcomen in 1712. It featured a single cylinder with a piston inside. When steam was let into the bottom of the cylinder, the piston was forced up, making a pump at the other end of a rocking beam go down. To bring the piston down and raise the pump, cold water had to be squirted into the cylinder to make the steam condense.

In 1765, about three months before Robert Fulton was born, Watt changed that. By directing the steam into a separate chamber and condensing it there, he produced an engine that would save energy and achieve greater power.

Always for Kathleen
S. K.

For my wife, Deborah,
and my daughters, Allison and Caitlin
B. F.

Text copyright © 1999 by Steven Kroll
Illustrations copyright © 1999 by Bill Farnsworth
ALL RIGHTS RESERVED
Printed in the United States of America
FIRST EDITION

Library of Congress Cataloging-in-Publication Data
Kroll, Steven.
Robert Fulton: from submarine to steamboat / by
Steven Kroll; illustrated by Bill Farnsworth.
— 1st ed. p. cm.
Summary: Describes the life and work of the
inventor who developed the steamboat and made it
a commercial success.
ISBN 0-8234-1433-7
1. Fulton, Robert, 1765–1815—Juvenile literature.
2. Marine engineers—United States—Biography—
Juvenile literature. 3. Inventors—United States—
Biography—Juvenile literature. 4. Steamboats—
United States—History—19th century—Juvenile
literature [1. Fulton, Robert, 1765–1815.
2. Inventors. 3. Steamboats—History.]
I. Farnsworth, Bill, ill. II. Title.
VM140.F9K76 1999
623.8'24'092—dc21
[B] 98-29944
CIP
AC